BATS

VAMPIRE BATS

Pamela J. Gerholdt
ABDO & Daughters

Published by Abdo & Daughters, 4940 Viking Drive, Suite 622, Edina, Minnesota 55435.

Library bound edition distributed by Rockbottom Books, Pentagon Tower, P.O. Box 36036, Minneapolis, Minnesota 55435.

Printed in the United States.

Cover Photo credit: Peter Arnold, Inc.
Interior Photo credits: Animals, Animals pages 7, 11
Bat Conservation International, Merlin D. Tuttle pages 5, 9, 13, 15, 19
Peter Arnold, Inc. pages 17, 21

Edited by Julie Berg

Library of Congress Cataloging-in-Publication Data

Gerholdt, Pamela J.
  Vampire bat / Pamela J. Gerholdt.
    p. cm. — (Bats)
Includes bibliographical references (p.23) and index.
ISBN 1-56239-505-X
1. Desmodus rotundus—Juvenile literature. 2. Vampire bats -Juvenile litera-
ture. [1. Vampire bats. 2. Bats.] I. Title. II. Series: Gerholdt, Pamela J. Bats.
QL737.C52G47 1995
599.4—dc20   95-8115
                                                                  CIP
                                                                  AC

About The Author

Pam Gerholdt has had a lifelong interest in animals. She is a member of the Minnesota Herpetological Society and is active in conservation issues. She lives in Webster, Minnesota with her husband, sons, and assorted other animals.

Contents

VAMPIRE BATS

There are over 900 **species** of bats in the world. Bats are **mammals** like dogs, cats, horses, and humans. But bats do something no other mammal can do—they can fly!

Vampire bats are called "New World" leaf-nosed bats because they are found in Central and South America. As their name suggests, vampire bats drink blood. But they aren't the scary creatures shown in movies and books.

Vampire bats have long, slender wings. They have brown fur on their heads and bellies which are lighter colored.

WHERE THEY'RE FOUND

Bats live on all of the world's **continents** except Antarctica, the **polar regions**, and a few ocean islands. Vampire bats live in Mexico, Chile, Argentina, Uruguay, and the islands of Margarita and Trinidad. Vampire bats do not live in central Europe where the stories about **vampires** and Dracula began.

Mexico

Margarita

Trinidad

Chile

Uruguay

Argentina

DETAIL AREA

Bats can be found on nearly every continent in the world. These flying fox bats are roosting in a tree in Borneo.

WHERE THEY LIVE

Vampire bats live in dry and wet areas, in yards, **pastures**, and all types of forests. They **roost** in caves, hollow trees, old wells, mine shafts, and abandoned buildings. These roosts usually have a strong **ammonia** smell from pools of **digested** blood.

If disturbed while roosting, vampire bats quickly fly into more protected areas of the roost. Vampire bats may roost alone, in small groups, or in **colonies** of 100 to over 2,000 bats.

Bats roost by hanging upside down by their feet. It's easy for them since they have 5 toes with sharp, curved claws, and knees that point backwards!

Vampire bats may roost alone or in small colonies by hanging upside down by their feet.

SIZES

Most bats are 3 to 5 inches (7.5 to 12.5 cm) long and weigh 1 to 3 ounces (28 to 98 g). But vampire bats only grow 2 to 2.5 inches (5 to 6.25 cm) long with a **wing span** of 12.5 to 14 inches (25 to 35 cm), and weigh .5 to 1.75 ounces (15 to 50 g).

Some bats are smaller than the vampire bat. The Kitti's hog-nosed bat is 1 inch (2.5 cm) long—about the size of a large bumble bee!

The large fruit-eating bats, such as flying foxes, can grow to over 16 inches (40 cm) long with a wing span over 5.5 feet (165 cm)!

A fruit-eating bat from Australia. With a wing span of up to 5 feet, it is much larger than the vampire bat.

SHAPES

Bats come in many different shapes. Vampire bats have small heads with short **snouts**. They have pointed ears and big eyes.

Most bats have short tails. A few, like the rat-tailed bats, have long tails. Vampire bats don't have any tail at all! Their wings are long and narrow. They are good for flying fast in the open areas where they find their food.

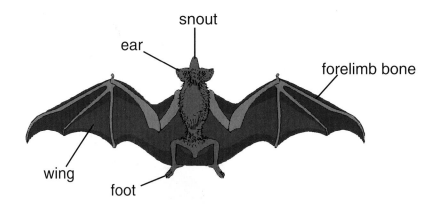

snout

ear

forelimb bone

wing

foot

Vampire bats have small heads with short snouts, pointed ears, and large eyes.

Bats' wings are made of their extra long fingers and **forelimb** bones that support thin, **elastic membranes**. Two membranes, top and bottom, are sandwiched together over the bones on each wing.

SENSES

Vampire bats have the same 5 senses as humans. Like over half of all bat **species**, they also use **echolocation** to "see" in the dark with sound.

Most bats that use echolocation send out squeaks or clicks from their mouths. Some, like the leaf-nosed bats, send sound out through their nostrils.

HOW ECHOLOCATION WORKS

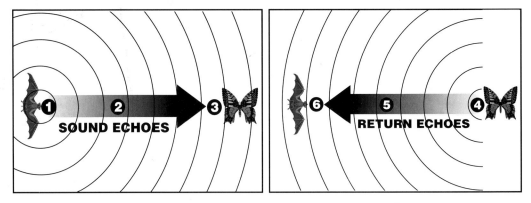

The bat sends out sound echoes (1). These echoes travel in all directions through the air (2). The sound echoes reach an object in the bat's path (3), then bounce off it (4). The return echoes travel through the air (5) and reach the bat (6). These echoes let the bat know where the object is, how large it is, and how fast it is moving.

Vampire bats use echolocation to "see" in the dark.

The vampire bat has a heat sensor on its nose. This helps it find an area on its **prey** where the blood flows close to the skin.

DEFENSE

Because they are small, vampire bats are "bite-sized" for many different kinds of **predators**. Cats, dogs, raccoons, and skunks eat bats. So do owls, hawks, falcons, snakes, and large frogs. Large spiders eat bats that get caught in their webs. Even worse, some bats eat other bats! The bats' best defense is to fly away.

Like most bats, vampire bats are **nocturnal**. This means they fly at night, avoiding many predators that hunt by day.

Bats also find safe, dark places to hide during the day when they **roost**. Vampire bats' dark color makes it hard for predators to see them in the dark.

*Vampire bats fly at night, avoiding most of their
enemies that move by day.*

FOOD

Vampire bats usually feed on the blood of sleeping horses, cattle, turkeys, and chickens. They can hear the regular breathing sounds of sleeping animals.

Using the heat sensor on its nose, the bat finds a place where the blood flows close to the animal's skin. Then it uses its razor-sharp front teeth to make a quick, round cut in the skin—about .2 inches (5 mm) deep and wide. The bat then licks the blood from the wound. It does not suck the blood through **fangs**.

A vampire bat needs about 2 tablespoons of blood every night. Vampire bats seem to be "one-stop shoppers," feeding on one animal a night.

Vampire bats feed on blood. This vampire bat is licking blood from a turkey's foot.

BABIES

Because bats fly, most people think bats are birds that lay eggs. But since bats are **mammals**, their babies are born live like humans.

Vampire bats **breed** once or twice a year, usually having one baby each time. The babies are well-developed at birth, with their eyes open. They are big when they are born, often weighing 25 percent of their mother's weight.

Female vampire bats take good care of their babies. At first, the babies drink their mother's milk. At 4 months old, the babies hunt for themselves. But they also get food from their mothers until they are 9 to 10 months old—6 months longer than most bats.

Young vampire bats hanging from a rock.

GLOSSARY

AMMONIA - A colorless gas that has a strong smell.

BREED - To produce young; also, a kind or type of animal.

COLONY - A group of living things of the same kind living together.

CONTINENT (KAHN-tih-nent) - One of the 7 main land masses: Europe, Asia, Africa, North America, South America, Australia and Antarctica.

DIGEST - To change food in the stomach and intestines so that the body can use it.

ECHOLOCATION (ek-o-lo-KAY-shun) - The use of sound waves to find objects.

ELASTIC (e-LAS-tik) - Able to return to its normal shape after being stretched or bent.

FANG - A long pointed tooth of an animal.

FORELIMB - A front limb of an animal.

MAMMALS (MAM-elz) - Animals with backbones that nurse their young.

MEMBRANES (MEM-branz) - Thin, easily bent layers of animal tissue.

NOCTURNAL (nok-TUR-nul) - Active by night.

PASTURE - A field where animals graze.

POLAR REGION - Of or near the North or South Pole.

PREDATOR (PRED-uh-tor) - An animal that eats other animals.

PREY - An animal hunted or found, and eaten by other animals.

ROOST - A place, such as a cave or tree, where bats rest during the day; also, to perch.

SNOUT - The nose and jaws of an animal.

SPECIES (SPEE-seas) - A kind or type of animal.

VAMPIRE - A mythical creature that comes to life at night and sucks blood from people while they sleep.

WING SPAN - The distance from the tip of one outstretched wing to the other.

BIBLIOGRAPHY

Fenton, M. Brock. *Bats.* Facts On File, Inc., 1992.

Findley, James S. *Bats, A Community Perspective.* Cambridge University Press, 1993.

Johnson, Sylvia A. *The World Of Bats.* Lerner Publications Company, 1985.

Nowak, Ronald M. *Walker's Bats Of The World.* The Johns Hopkins University Press, 1994.

Index